THE
VLOGGER AI

Utilize The Use of Artificial Intelligence To Craft Compelling Content and Build Authentic Business Online

Calista Moon

All rights reserved. No part of this book may be reproduced, distributed, or transmitted in any form or by any means, including photocopying, recording, or other electronic or mechanical methods, without the prior written permission of the copyright owner except in the case of brief quotations embodied in critical reviews and certain other noncommercial uses permitted by copyright.

Copyright © 2024 by Calista Moon

Table of Contents

Introduction 5

Chapter 1: The Genesis of VLOGGER AI 9

Chapter 2: Exploring the Technology Behind VLOGGER AI 14

Chapter 3: Delving into VLOGGER AI's Functionality 19

Chapter 4: Limitations and Challenges of VLOGGER AI 25

Chapter 5: Transforming Content Creation with VLOGGER AI 32

Chapter 6: Ethical Considerations in AI-driven Content Creation 38

Chapter 7: The Power of Diffusion Models in Avatar Animation 43

Chapter 8: Leveraging the MENTOR Dataset ... 48

Chapter 9: Comparative Analysis 54

Chapter 10: Regulatory Frameworks and Policies 60

Chapter 11: Future Trends: The Evolution of VLOGGER AI............ 65

Chapter 12: Societal Impacts and Cultural Shifts 71

Conclusion............ 77

Introduction

Welcome to the exciting world of VLOGGER AI, where innovation meets creativity, and the possibilities are endless. In this book, we embark on a journey of exploration, delving deep into the transformative power of artificial intelligence in content creation. From its genesis to its real-world applications, from its technological underpinnings to its societal implications, we leave no stone unturned as we unravel the mysteries of VLOGGER AI.

As developers at Google continue to push the boundaries of what is possible with AI technology, VLOGGER stands out as a groundbreaking innovation—a tool that seamlessly transforms still images into dynamic videos, complete with lifelike animations and facial expressions. But VLOGGER is more than just a technological marvel; it represents a paradigm shift in the way we create, consume, and interact with digital media.

Our journey begins with an overview of VLOGGER AI, providing readers with a comprehensive understanding of its capabilities, limitations, and potential impact. We explore the genesis of VLOGGER, tracing its origins back to the pioneering efforts of Google's research teams and the evolution of diffusion models in avatar animation.

From there, we delve into the technology behind VLOGGER AI, offering readers an in-depth exploration of the underlying algorithms, neural networks, and computational processes that power this revolutionary tool. We examine the role of diffusion models in avatar animation, the training process leveraging the MENTOR dataset, and the real-world applications that showcase the true potential of VLOGGER AI.

But our journey does not end there. We also confront the ethical considerations and regulatory frameworks surrounding AI-driven content creation, exploring topics such as data privacy, intellectual property rights, and ethical guidelines. We examine the societal impacts and cultural shifts brought about by VLOGGER AI, considering its implications for diversity, representation, and inclusivity in digital media.

As we navigate the complexities of VLOGGER AI, one thing becomes clear: the conversation is just beginning. In this rapidly evolving landscape, it is essential to stay informed, engaged, and proactive in shaping the future of AI-driven content creation. Whether you are a seasoned technologist, a budding content creator, or simply curious about the intersection of technology and creativity, there is something for everyone in the pages that follow.

So, I invite you to join me on this journey into the world of VLOGGER AI. Together, let us explore the possibilities, confront the challenges, and embrace the opportunities that lie ahead. The future of content creation is here, and it is more exciting than ever before.

Chapter 1: The Genesis of VLOGGER AI

In the ever-evolving landscape of artificial intelligence, Google's VLOGGER AI emerges as a pioneering creation, reshaping how we interact with digital avatars and multimedia content. This section delves into the genesis of VLOGGER AI, tracing its origins, development process, and the innovative technologies that underpin its functionality.

Origins of VLOGGER AI

VLOGGER AI traces its origins to Google's ambitious research initiatives in artificial intelligence, driven by the goal of pushing the boundaries of what AI can achieve in content creation and virtual communication. The inception of VLOGGER AI can be attributed to Google's dedication to innovation and its commitment to leveraging AI for positive societal impact.

Development Process

The development of VLOGGER AI involved a multidisciplinary approach, bringing together experts in machine learning, computer vision, natural language processing, and multimedia processing. Google's research teams collaborated closely to design and implement the complex algorithms and models that power VLOGGER AI's avatar animation capabilities.

From conceptualization to implementation, the development process spanned multiple phases, including data collection and preprocessing, algorithm design, model training, and iterative testing and refinement. Google's rigorous approach to research and development ensured that VLOGGER AI met high standards of performance, reliability, and user experience.

Innovative Technologies

At the heart of VLOGGER AI lies a convergence of innovative technologies, each contributing to its remarkable capabilities in avatar animation and content synthesis. One key technology is diffusion models, which enable VLOGGER AI to generate realistic facial expressions, gestures, and movements based on input data.

Diffusion models leverage advanced machine learning techniques to capture complex patterns and dynamics in data, allowing VLOGGER AI to synthesize lifelike animations with unprecedented fidelity. Additionally, VLOGGER AI incorporates state-of-the-art algorithms for image processing, audio analysis, and natural language understanding, further enhancing its versatility and adaptability.

Furthermore, VLOGGER AI leverages advancements in neural network architectures, training methodologies, and computational infrastructure to achieve real-time performance and scalability. Google's investment in cutting-edge research and development ensures that VLOGGER AI remains at the forefront of AI-driven content creation technology.

Impact and Implications

The genesis of VLOGGER AI marks a significant milestone in the evolution of artificial intelligence, with profound implications for various industries and sectors. By democratizing content creation and virtual communication, VLOGGER AI empowers individuals and organizations to express themselves creatively, connect with audiences authentically, and explore new possibilities in digital storytelling.

Moreover, VLOGGER AI has the potential to revolutionize industries such as marketing, entertainment, education, and beyond, unlocking new opportunities for innovation, engagement, and personalization. As VLOGGER AI continues to evolve and mature, its impact on society, culture, and technology will be increasingly profound, shaping the future of human-computer interaction and digital expression.

Chapter 2: Exploring the Technology Behind VLOGGER AI

VLOGGER AI, developed by Google, stands at the forefront of AI-driven content creation, revolutionizing the way we interact with multimedia. In this section, we delve into the intricate technology powering VLOGGER AI, unraveling its core components and mechanisms.

Understanding Neural Networks and Deep Learning

At the heart of VLOGGER AI lies a sophisticated neural network architecture fueled by deep learning algorithms. Neural networks mimic the structure and function of the human brain, comprising interconnected nodes, or neurons, organized into layers. These networks learn from vast datasets, adjusting their parameters to optimize performance over time.

Leveraging Generative Models for Realistic Output

VLOGGER AI harnesses the power of generative models, particularly diffusion models, to produce lifelike video content from still images. Diffusion models excel at generating high-quality samples by iteratively diffusing noise into the data space. This approach ensures realistic output while preserving the integrity of the original input.

Real-time Facial Expression Synthesis

One of VLOGGER AI's standout features is its ability to synthesize facial expressions in real-time. By analyzing facial landmarks and leveraging advanced computer vision techniques, the AI accurately replicates nuanced expressions, capturing the subtleties of human emotion with remarkable precision.

Dynamic Avatar Animation

VLOGGER AI goes beyond static avatars, breathing life into digital characters through dynamic animation. Using predictive modeling and motion capture technology, the AI imbues avatars with fluid movements and natural gestures, enhancing their realism and expressiveness.

Personalized Content Creation Tools

Central to VLOGGER AI's appeal is its suite of personalized content creation tools, tailored to meet the diverse needs of users. Whether generating marketing videos, educational content, or virtual presentations, the AI empowers individuals and organizations to unleash their creativity and captivate audiences.

Advancements in Natural Language Processing

In addition to visual content creation, VLOGGER AI boasts advanced natural language processing capabilities, enabling seamless integration of voiceovers and scripted dialogue. By analyzing audio inputs and synthesizing speech in real-time, the AI delivers compelling narratives that complement its visual output.

Optimizing Computational Resources for Efficiency

Despite its computational complexity, VLOGGER AI optimizes resource utilization to deliver fast and efficient performance. Through parallel processing, distributed computing, and hardware acceleration, the AI minimizes latency and maximizes throughput, ensuring a smooth user experience even on resource-constrained devices.

Enhancing User Interactivity and Engagement

Beyond traditional content creation tools, VLOGGER AI prioritizes user interactivity and engagement, fostering meaningful interactions between creators and their audiences. With features like interactive avatars and customizable animations, the AI enables immersive storytelling experiences that captivate and inspire.

Chapter 3: Delving into VLOGGER AI's Functionality

VLOGGER AI, developed by Google, represents a paradigm shift in content creation, offering users unprecedented capabilities to transform still images into dynamic videos. In this section, we explore the multifaceted functionality of VLOGGER AI, dissecting its core features and workflows.

Image Processing and Analysis

At the core of VLOGGER AI's functionality lies its advanced image processing and analysis capabilities. Upon receiving a still image input, the AI meticulously examines every pixel, identifying key facial landmarks, expressions, and features. Through state-of-the-art computer vision algorithms, VLOGGER AI extracts valuable information to inform its subsequent actions.

Audio-to-Video Synthesis

A hallmark feature of VLOGGER AI is its ability to synthesize lifelike video content from audio inputs. Leveraging cutting-edge deep learning techniques, the AI seamlessly aligns audio tracks with corresponding facial movements, lip-syncing dialogue with remarkable accuracy. This process involves mapping phonetic sounds to visual cues, ensuring coherence between audio and video elements.

Facial Expression Generation

VLOGGER AI excels at generating realistic facial expressions, infusing digital avatars with emotive qualities that mirror human behavior. By analyzing speech patterns, intonations, and contextual cues, the AI dynamically adjusts facial muscles to reflect the speaker's emotions and intentions. From subtle smiles to pronounced frowns, VLOGGER AI captures the full spectrum of human expression.

Motion Dynamics and Animation

In addition to facial expressions, VLOGGER AI orchestrates fluid motion dynamics and animations, bringing characters to life with cinematic flair. Through a combination of physics-based simulation and motion capture data, the AI imbues avatars with natural movements and gestures, enhancing their believability and expressiveness. Whether delivering a presentation or starring in a marketing campaign, VLOGGER AI ensures that characters move with grace and authenticity.

Real-time Rendering and Optimization

To deliver a seamless user experience, VLOGGER AI employs real-time rendering techniques and optimization strategies. By leveraging hardware acceleration and parallel processing, the AI minimizes latency and maximizes frame rates, ensuring smooth playback and responsiveness. This optimization extends to resource management, dynamically adjusting rendering parameters to accommodate varying hardware configurations.

Customization and Personalization Tools

Recognizing the diverse needs of content creators, VLOGGER AI offers a suite of customization and personalization tools. From adjusting facial features to fine-tuning animation styles, users have granular control over every aspect of their creations. This level of customization empowers individuals and businesses to tailor content to specific audiences and objectives, fostering deeper engagement and resonance.

Integration with External Platforms and Software

VLOGGER AI seamlessly integrates with external platforms and software ecosystems, facilitating interoperability and collaboration. Whether exporting videos to social media channels or importing assets from third-party applications, the AI streamlines workflows and enhances productivity. This interoperability extends to data exchange protocols and APIs, enabling seamless communication between VLOGGER AI and external systems.

Continuous Learning and Improvement

As a testament to Google's commitment to innovation, VLOGGER AI undergoes continuous learning and improvement. Through feedback loops and iterative refinement processes, the AI evolves over time, adapting to changing user preferences and technological advancements. This commitment to excellence ensures that VLOGGER AI remains at the forefront of content creation technology, delivering cutting-edge solutions to its users.

Chapter 4: Limitations and Challenges of VLOGGER AI

While VLOGGER AI represents a significant advancement in content creation technology, it is not without its limitations and challenges. In this section, we delve into the various factors that constrain the capabilities of VLOGGER AI and the obstacles it faces in achieving widespread adoption.

Computational Resource Requirements

One of the primary limitations of VLOGGER AI lies in its demanding computational resource requirements. The complex algorithms and neural networks used to generate lifelike videos require substantial processing power and memory bandwidth. As a result, users may encounter performance bottlenecks when running VLOGGER AI on hardware with limited capabilities. High-end graphics processing units (GPUs) and central processing units (CPUs) are often necessary to achieve real-time rendering and smooth playback, posing challenges for users with budget constraints or outdated hardware.

Data Availability and Quality

The effectiveness of VLOGGER AI is heavily reliant on the availability and quality of training data. While Google has access to vast datasets containing diverse images and videos, the generalizability of these datasets may be limited in certain contexts. In scenarios where specific demographic groups or cultural nuances are underrepresented, VLOGGER AI may struggle to produce accurate and culturally sensitive content. Additionally, issues related to data bias and fairness can undermine the ethical integrity of VLOGGER AI, raising concerns about the perpetuation of stereotypes and discriminatory practices in content generation.

Ethical Considerations and Misuse

The rise of deepfake technology, of which VLOGGER AI is a notable example, has raised profound ethical concerns regarding its potential for misuse and deception. While VLOGGER AI is intended for legitimate content creation purposes, there is a risk that malicious actors may exploit its capabilities to create misleading or harmful content. From impersonating public figures to spreading disinformation and propaganda, the misuse of VLOGGER AI poses significant challenges for content moderation and trust in digital media. Addressing these ethical considerations requires a multifaceted approach, involving collaboration between technology companies, policymakers, and civil society organizations to develop robust safeguards and accountability mechanisms.

Legal and Regulatory Compliance

As with any AI-driven technology, VLOGGER AI must adhere to legal and regulatory frameworks governing data privacy, intellectual property rights, and content moderation. However, navigating the complex landscape of regulations and compliance requirements can be daunting for both developers and users of VLOGGER AI. Ensuring compliance with applicable laws and regulations, such as the General Data Protection Regulation (GDPR) in the European Union and the Digital Millennium Copyright Act (DMCA) in the United States, requires a thorough understanding of legal obligations and best practices. Failure to comply with these regulations can result in legal liabilities and reputational damage, posing significant challenges for the widespread adoption of VLOGGER AI in commercial and consumer contexts.

User Experience and Accessibility

While VLOGGER AI offers powerful capabilities for content creation, its user experience and accessibility may vary depending on the skill level and technical expertise of the user. Novice users may find the interface and controls of VLOGGER AI daunting or unintuitive, hindering their ability to fully leverage its features. Additionally, individuals with disabilities or impairments may encounter barriers to access and participation in content creation activities facilitated by VLOGGER AI. Ensuring a seamless and inclusive user experience requires ongoing efforts to improve usability, provide comprehensive documentation and tutorials, and incorporate accessibility features that accommodate diverse user needs.

Cultural and Linguistic Diversity

VLOGGER AI's effectiveness in generating accurate and culturally relevant content is contingent on its ability to accommodate diverse cultural and linguistic contexts. However, achieving this level of cultural and linguistic diversity presents significant challenges, as cultural norms, linguistic nuances, and regional accents vary widely across different populations and geographic regions. Ensuring that VLOGGER AI can accurately capture and represent this diversity requires extensive research, data collection, and algorithmic refinement. Moreover, addressing cultural and linguistic biases in AI systems is an ongoing process that requires collaboration with experts from diverse backgrounds and communities to identify and mitigate sources of bias and discrimination.

Chapter 5: Transforming Content Creation with VLOGGER AI

VLOGGER AI represents a groundbreaking leap in content creation technology, revolutionizing the way multimedia content is produced and consumed. In this section, we explore the transformative impact of VLOGGER AI across various industries and sectors, highlighting its potential to reshape the landscape of digital media and communication.

Enhancing Creativity and Expression

One of the most significant contributions of VLOGGER AI to content creation is its ability to enhance creativity and expression. By enabling users to generate lifelike videos from still images and audio clips, VLOGGER AI unlocks new avenues for storytelling and visual communication. Creators can now bring their ideas to life with unprecedented realism, imbuing their content with emotion, personality, and authenticity. Whether it's producing animated shorts, promotional videos, or personalized messages, VLOGGER AI empowers creators to unleash their creativity and connect with audiences in meaningful ways.

Streamlining Production Workflows

VLOGGER AI streamlines the content production process, reducing the time, effort, and resources required to create high-quality multimedia content. Traditional video production workflows typically involve complex equipment, specialized skills, and labor-intensive editing processes. With VLOGGER AI, much of this complexity is eliminated, allowing users to generate professional-looking videos with minimal input. Whether it's automating lip-syncing, facial animation, or scene composition, VLOGGER AI accelerates the production timeline and enables rapid iteration, facilitating agile content creation in dynamic environments.

Personalizing User Experiences

Personalization is a key driver of engagement and satisfaction in today's digital landscape, and VLOGGER AI offers powerful capabilities for tailoring content to individual preferences and interests. By analyzing user data and behavior, VLOGGER AI can dynamically adapt content to match user preferences, demographics, and viewing habits. Whether it's customizing marketing messages, educational materials, or entertainment content, VLOGGER AI enables personalized user experiences that resonate with audiences on a deeper level. From interactive storytelling to adaptive learning environments, the possibilities for personalization are virtually limitless with VLOGGER AI.

Democratizing Access to Media Production

One of the most democratizing aspects of VLOGGER AI is its ability to democratize access to media production tools and techniques. Historically, content creation has been dominated by large studios, production companies, and skilled professionals with access to specialized equipment and training. With VLOGGER AI, however, anyone with a smartphone or computer can become a content creator, regardless of their background or expertise. This democratization of content creation empowers individuals and communities to tell their own stories, share their perspectives, and participate in global conversations, fostering greater diversity and inclusivity in media representation.

Fostering Innovation and Experimentation

VLOGGER AI fosters a culture of innovation and experimentation in content creation, encouraging users to explore new formats, styles, and genres. By providing access to cutting-edge technology and tools, VLOGGER AI inspires creators to push the boundaries of traditional media and embrace unconventional approaches to storytelling. From augmented reality experiences to interactive narratives, VLOGGER AI opens up new frontiers for creative expression and artistic experimentation, fueling a renaissance of digital media innovation.

Amplifying Brand Engagement and Impact

For businesses and organizations, VLOGGER AI offers unparalleled opportunities to amplify brand engagement and impact through immersive, interactive content experiences. By harnessing the power of VLOGGER AI, brands can create compelling narratives, authentic spokespersons, and memorable brand ambassadors that resonate with consumers on a personal level. Whether it's producing engaging advertisements, informative tutorials, or entertaining social media content, VLOGGER AI enables brands to connect with audiences in ways that traditional advertising cannot, driving brand awareness, loyalty, and advocacy.

Chapter 6: Ethical Considerations in AI-driven Content Creation

As AI-driven technologies like VLOGGER AI continue to advance, it is essential to examine the ethical implications of their use in content creation. While these technologies offer unprecedented opportunities for creativity and innovation, they also raise important ethical considerations that must be addressed to ensure responsible and equitable deployment. In this section, we explore the ethical considerations surrounding AI-driven content creation and the principles that guide ethical decision-making in this evolving landscape.

1. Data Privacy and Security

One of the foremost ethical considerations in AI-driven content creation is data privacy and security. As AI algorithms rely on vast amounts of data to generate content, ensuring the privacy and security of user data is paramount. Organizations must implement robust data protection measures, such as encryption, access controls, and anonymization techniques, to safeguard sensitive information from unauthorized access, misuse, and exploitation. Additionally, transparent data collection practices and informed consent mechanisms are essential to empower users to make informed decisions about how their data is used and shared.

2. Bias and Fairness

Another critical ethical consideration is bias and fairness in AI-driven content creation. AI algorithms are susceptible to bias, reflecting the biases inherent in the data they are trained on and the design decisions made by their creators. Biased content can perpetuate harmful stereotypes, reinforce inequalities, and marginalize underrepresented groups. To address bias and promote fairness, organizations must strive to ensure diverse and representative datasets, implement bias detection and mitigation techniques, and incorporate principles of fairness, accountability, and transparency into the design and development of AI systems.

3. Transparency and Accountability

Transparency and accountability are essential principles in AI-driven content creation. Users have a right to know when they are interacting with AI-generated content and to understand how it was created and by whom. Organizations must be transparent about the use of AI technologies in content creation, providing clear disclosures and explanations to users about the capabilities and limitations of AI-generated content. Additionally, establishing mechanisms for accountability, such as auditing, monitoring, and reporting processes, can help mitigate risks and ensure responsible use of AI technologies in content creation.

4. Intellectual Property Rights

Intellectual property rights are another important ethical consideration in AI-driven content creation. As AI technologies generate increasingly sophisticated and original content, questions arise about ownership, attribution, and licensing rights. Organizations must navigate complex legal and ethical frameworks to ensure that AI-generated content respects the intellectual property rights of creators, collaborators, and original content sources. Clear guidelines and agreements outlining ownership, usage rights, and attribution requirements can help clarify responsibilities and prevent disputes over ownership and authorship of AI-generated content.

5. Societal Impact and Responsibility

Finally, AI-driven content creation has broader societal implications that must be considered. Organizations have a responsibility to assess the potential social, cultural, and economic impacts of AI-generated content and to prioritize the well-being and interests of all stakeholders. This includes addressing concerns about job displacement, automation, and the concentration of power and influence in the hands of a few technology companies. By adopting a holistic approach to ethical decision-making, organizations can promote inclusivity, diversity, and social responsibility in AI-driven content creation, ensuring that the benefits of these technologies are shared equitably across society.

Chapter 7: The Power of Diffusion Models in Avatar Animation

Avatar animation has undergone a revolution with the emergence of diffusion models, paving the way for lifelike and dynamic representations of individuals in digital environments. In this section, we delve into the intricacies of diffusion models and explore their transformative impact on avatar animation.

Understanding Diffusion Models

Diffusion models, also known as generative models, are a class of artificial intelligence algorithms that excel in capturing complex patterns and generating realistic outputs. Unlike traditional models that rely on predefined rules or templates, diffusion models learn directly from data, enabling them to produce highly detailed and naturalistic representations of phenomena. These models leverage advanced statistical techniques, such as probabilistic modeling and deep learning, to simulate the diffusion process and generate realistic samples.

Advantages of Diffusion Models in Avatar Animation

The application of diffusion models in avatar animation offers several distinct advantages over traditional approaches. Firstly, diffusion models excel in capturing the nuances of human appearance and behavior, resulting in more authentic and expressive avatars. By analyzing vast amounts of training data, including images, videos, and motion sequences, diffusion models can learn to generate avatars with realistic facial features, expressions, and movements, enhancing the overall believability and immersion of virtual characters.

Secondly, diffusion models enable personalized avatar creation, allowing users to customize their digital representations based on their unique characteristics and preferences. Whether it's adjusting facial features, hairstyles, or clothing styles, diffusion models can adapt to individual input and generate avatars that closely resemble their real-life counterparts. This level of customization enhances user engagement and immersion, fostering a deeper connection between users and their digital personas.

Applications of Diffusion Models in Avatar Animation

The versatility of diffusion models extends beyond entertainment and gaming, finding applications in various domains, including virtual communication, education, and healthcare. In virtual communication platforms, diffusion models enable users to interact with lifelike avatars that accurately reflect their emotions and gestures, enhancing the quality and authenticity of remote interactions. In education, diffusion models facilitate immersive learning experiences by creating virtual tutors and mentors that engage and instruct students in personalized ways. In healthcare, diffusion models can be used to develop virtual patients for medical training and simulation, enabling healthcare professionals to practice clinical skills and procedures in a realistic and risk-free environment.

Challenges and Future Directions

While diffusion models hold great promise for avatar animation, they also pose challenges and limitations that must be addressed. One such challenge is the computational complexity and resource requirements associated with training and deploying diffusion models, particularly for high-resolution and real-time applications. Additionally, ensuring diversity and inclusivity in avatar representation remains an ongoing challenge, as diffusion models may inadvertently perpetuate biases and stereotypes present in the training data.

Looking ahead, future research in avatar animation will focus on overcoming these challenges and advancing the capabilities of diffusion models. This includes exploring novel training techniques, improving model scalability and efficiency, and developing frameworks for ethical and responsible AI design. By harnessing the power of diffusion models and pushing the boundaries of avatar animation, researchers and practitioners can unlock new possibilities for immersive and interactive digital experiences.

Chapter 8: Leveraging the MENTOR Dataset

Training artificial intelligence models such as VLOGGER requires vast amounts of high-quality data to learn from. In the case of VLOGGER, Google leverages the MENTOR dataset, a comprehensive collection of diverse portraits and videos, to train the AI model. This section delves into the significance of the MENTOR dataset, the training process of VLOGGER, and the implications of leveraging such extensive data for AI development.

Understanding the MENTOR Dataset

The MENTOR dataset serves as a cornerstone for training VLOGGER, providing the AI model with a rich and diverse source of visual and auditory information. Comprising over 800,000 portraits and more than 2,200 hours of videos, the MENTOR dataset offers unparalleled breadth and depth in terms of demographic diversity, facial expressions, and social contexts. This extensive dataset encompasses a wide range of subjects, including individuals of different races, ages, genders, and cultural backgrounds, ensuring that VLOGGER can generate realistic avatars that reflect the diversity of human appearance and behavior.

Importance of Diverse Data

The diversity of the MENTOR dataset is crucial for training VLOGGER to accurately capture the nuances of human expression and behavior. By exposing the AI model to a wide variety of visual and auditory stimuli, including different facial features, expressions, accents, and speech patterns, the MENTOR dataset enables VLOGGER to generalize and adapt to novel scenarios and individuals. This diversity not only enhances the realism and authenticity of the generated avatars but also mitigates the risk of bias and discrimination in AI-generated content.

Insights into the Training Process

The training process of VLOGGER involves feeding the MENTOR dataset into the AI model and iteratively optimizing its parameters to minimize the discrepancy between the generated avatars and the ground truth images and videos. This process, known as supervised learning, relies on advanced machine learning algorithms, such as convolutional neural networks (CNNs) and recurrent neural networks (RNNs), to extract meaningful features from the input data and generate accurate predictions. Additionally, techniques such as data augmentation, regularization, and transfer learning are employed to enhance the robustness and generalization capabilities of the AI model.

Challenges and Considerations

While the MENTOR dataset provides a wealth of training data for VLOGGER, its sheer size and complexity pose several challenges and considerations. Managing and processing large-scale datasets require significant computational resources and infrastructure, including high-performance computing clusters and specialized hardware accelerators. Furthermore, ensuring the privacy and security of sensitive information contained within the dataset is paramount, necessitating robust data anonymization and access controls to prevent unauthorized use or disclosure.

Ethical and Societal Implications

The use of the MENTOR dataset raises important ethical and societal considerations regarding data privacy, consent, and representation. As AI models like VLOGGER become increasingly proficient at generating lifelike avatars, questions arise about the ownership and control of the generated content, as well as its potential impact on individuals' privacy and autonomy. Additionally, the representation of diverse demographics in the dataset must be carefully curated to avoid perpetuating stereotypes or biases in the generated avatars.

Future Directions

Looking ahead, future research in AI and data science will continue to explore innovative approaches for collecting, curating, and leveraging large-scale datasets for AI training. This includes developing techniques for synthetic data generation, federated learning, and differential privacy to address the challenges of data scarcity, privacy preservation, and bias mitigation. By advancing the state-of-the-art in data-driven AI development, researchers can unlock new possibilities for creating intelligent systems that are equitable, inclusive, and ethically responsible.

Chapter 9: Comparative Analysis

In the rapidly evolving landscape of artificial intelligence (AI), VLOGGER AI stands out as a groundbreaking technology that revolutionizes content creation through lifelike avatar animation. As AI-driven applications continue to proliferate, it is essential to compare VLOGGER AI with similar technologies to understand its unique features, strengths, and limitations. This comparative analysis evaluates VLOGGER AI against other AI-driven content creation platforms, examining key aspects such as features, performance, and usability.

Understanding VLOGGER AI

VLOGGER AI, developed by Google, is a state-of-the-art AI model that transforms still images into dynamic videos featuring realistic avatars. Using advanced deep learning techniques, VLOGGER AI synthesizes facial expressions, gestures, and speech from input data, creating lifelike animations that mimic human behavior. With its seamless integration of image processing, natural language understanding, and animation synthesis, VLOGGER AI offers unparalleled capabilities for generating personalized content with minimal user input.

Comparative Platforms

Several other AI-driven content creation platforms exist in the market, each with its own unique features and functionalities. One such platform is DeepArt, which utilizes deep neural networks to generate artistic images and animations based on user input. While DeepArt excels in creating visually striking content, its focus on artistic expression may limit its suitability for creating realistic avatars or dynamic videos.

Another notable platform is Loom.ai, which specializes in creating 3D avatars from 2D images using computer vision and machine learning algorithms. Unlike VLOGGER AI, which focuses on video content generation, Loom.ai prioritizes avatar creation for virtual reality (VR) and augmented reality (AR) applications. While Loom.ai offers impressive avatar customization options and integration with VR/AR platforms, its scope may be narrower compared to VLOGGER AI's broader applicability in multimedia content creation.

Feature Comparison

When comparing VLOGGER AI with similar technologies, it is essential to consider their respective features and capabilities. VLOGGER AI distinguishes itself with its real-time facial expression synthesis, dynamic avatar animation, and personalized content creation capabilities. By analyzing audio-visual input data, VLOGGER AI accurately synchronizes lip movements, facial expressions, and body gestures, resulting in lifelike animations that resonate with viewers.

In contrast, other AI-driven content creation platforms may offer differentiating features such as style transfer, image-to-image translation, or scene generation. While these features may appeal to certain user demographics or use cases, they may lack the comprehensive functionality and versatility of VLOGGER AI in generating realistic human-like avatars and videos.

Performance Evaluation

Assessing the performance of VLOGGER AI and similar technologies involves evaluating various metrics such as output quality, processing speed, and resource efficiency. VLOGGER AI demonstrates impressive performance in generating high-fidelity animations with minimal input data, thanks to its sophisticated deep learning algorithms and extensive training data. With its efficient utilization of computational resources, VLOGGER AI delivers real-time responsiveness and scalability, making it suitable for a wide range of applications.

In comparison, other AI-driven content creation platforms may exhibit varying levels of performance depending on factors such as model complexity, dataset size, and algorithm efficiency. While some platforms may excel in specific tasks or domains, they may struggle with scalability, latency, or resource constraints, limiting their practical utility in real-world scenarios.

Usability and Accessibility

The usability and accessibility of VLOGGER AI play a crucial role in its adoption and integration into existing workflows. With its user-friendly interface, intuitive controls, and seamless integration with popular content creation tools, VLOGGER AI offers a streamlined user experience that empowers creators of all skill levels to produce compelling multimedia content. Moreover, Google's extensive documentation, developer support, and community resources further enhance the accessibility of VLOGGER AI, facilitating widespread adoption and innovation.

In contrast, other AI-driven content creation platforms may exhibit varying levels of usability and accessibility, depending on factors such as user interface design, documentation quality, and developer support. While some platforms may offer advanced customization options or specialized features, they may require steep learning curves or technical expertise to effectively utilize, limiting their accessibility to non-expert users.

Chapter 10: Regulatory Frameworks and Policies

In the fast-paced world of artificial intelligence (AI) and content creation, navigating regulatory frameworks and policies is crucial to ensuring ethical, responsible, and compliant use of AI technologies. This comprehensive exploration delves into the complex legal landscape surrounding AI-driven content creation, focusing on key aspects such as data privacy, intellectual property rights, and ethical guidelines.

Data Privacy Regulations

One of the primary considerations in AI-driven content creation is data privacy, as AI models often rely on large datasets containing sensitive information. Various regulatory frameworks, such as the General Data Protection Regulation

(GDPR) in the European Union and the California Consumer Privacy Act (CCPA) in the United States, mandate strict requirements for the collection, processing, and storage of personal data. Compliance with these regulations is essential for organizations developing and deploying AI technologies like VLOGGER AI, as non-compliance can result in significant fines and reputational damage.

Intellectual Property Rights

Intellectual property (IP) rights play a crucial role in AI-driven content creation, particularly concerning the ownership and use of generated content. As VLOGGER AI produces videos and animations based on input data, questions may arise regarding the ownership of the resulting content and the rights of individuals depicted in the generated media. Clear guidelines and agreements must be established to address issues such as copyright, licensing, and attribution, ensuring that creators, users, and subjects are adequately protected under existing IP laws.

Ethical Guidelines and Best Practices

Ethical considerations are paramount in AI-driven content creation, as the use of AI technologies can raise ethical concerns related to authenticity, representation, and manipulation. Industry organizations, research institutions, and governmental agencies have developed ethical guidelines and best practices to promote responsible AI development and deployment. For example, the IEEE Global Initiative on Ethics of Autonomous and Intelligent Systems has published Ethically Aligned Design principles, which advocate for transparency, accountability, and inclusivity in AI technologies. Adhering to these ethical guidelines is essential for developers, users, and stakeholders involved in AI-driven content creation to ensure that AI technologies are used in a manner that respects human dignity, diversity, and societal values.

Compliance and Risk Management

Compliance with regulatory frameworks and ethical guidelines requires a proactive approach to risk management and governance. Organizations developing and deploying AI-driven content creation technologies must establish robust compliance programs, risk assessment procedures, and governance structures to mitigate legal and ethical risks effectively. This includes conducting thorough impact assessments, implementing privacy-by-design principles, and establishing clear accountability mechanisms throughout the AI lifecycle. By integrating compliance and risk management into their AI development processes, organizations can build trust, foster transparency, and demonstrate their commitment to ethical AI practices.

International Collaboration and Standardization

Given the global nature of AI-driven content creation, international collaboration and standardization efforts are essential for harmonizing regulatory frameworks and promoting interoperability. Organizations such as the International Organization for Standardization (ISO) and the Partnership on AI (PAI) facilitate collaboration among stakeholders from industry, academia, and government to develop common standards, guidelines, and best practices for AI technologies. By participating in these collaborative initiatives, policymakers, regulators, and industry players can address regulatory gaps, promote innovation, and foster responsible AI adoption on a global scale.

Chapter 11: Future Trends: The Evolution of VLOGGER AI

As technology continues to advance at an unprecedented pace, the future evolution of VLOGGER AI holds immense promise for transforming the landscape of content creation. This in-depth exploration delves into the anticipated trends, developments, and innovations that are poised to shape the future trajectory of VLOGGER AI, offering insights into its potential impact on society, culture, and technology.

Advancements in AI Technology

One of the most significant trends driving the evolution of VLOGGER AI is the continued advancement of AI technology itself. As researchers and developers push the

65

boundaries of machine learning, deep learning, and natural language processing, VLOGGER AI stands to benefit from improved algorithms, models, and computational techniques. This includes enhancements in areas such as facial recognition, speech synthesis, and motion generation, enabling VLOGGER AI to produce even more realistic and immersive content.

Integration of Augmented Reality (AR) and Virtual Reality (VR)

The integration of augmented reality (AR) and virtual reality (VR) technologies is poised to revolutionize the way we interact with VLOGGER AI-generated content. By combining VLOGGER AI with AR/VR platforms, users can experience immersive storytelling, interactive simulations, and lifelike avatars in virtual environments. This convergence of technologies opens up new possibilities for entertainment, education, training, and communication, ushering in a new era of digital experiences that blur the lines between the virtual and physical worlds.

Personalized and Context-Aware Content Creation

As VLOGGER AI continues to mature, personalized and context-aware content creation is expected to become increasingly prevalent. By leveraging user data, preferences, and behaviors, VLOGGER AI can tailor content to individual needs, interests, and demographics, delivering highly relevant and engaging experiences. Whether it's personalized video messages, customized tutorials, or targeted advertising campaigns, VLOGGER AI has the potential to revolutionize the way content is created, consumed, and monetized across various industries and sectors.

Multi-Modal and Cross-Platform Integration

Another emerging trend in the evolution of VLOGGER AI is the integration of multi-modal capabilities and cross-platform compatibility. Rather than being limited to generating static videos or animations, future iterations of VLOGGER AI may incorporate additional modalities such as text, audio, and 3D graphics, enabling more dynamic and interactive content creation. Furthermore, VLOGGER AI may seamlessly integrate with existing platforms and ecosystems, allowing users to access and share content across a wide range of devices and channels with ease.

Ethical and Regulatory Considerations

As VLOGGER AI becomes more pervasive in our daily lives, ethical and regulatory considerations will play an increasingly critical role in shaping its future development and deployment. Concerns related to privacy, consent, bias, and accountability must be addressed to ensure that VLOGGER AI is used responsibly and ethically. Policymakers, regulators, and industry stakeholders will need to collaborate closely to establish clear guidelines, standards, and best practices that promote the responsible use of AI technologies while safeguarding individual rights and societal values.

Societal Impact and Cultural Implications

The evolution of VLOGGER AI is not only reshaping the way we create and consume content but also influencing societal norms, cultural practices, and collective consciousness. As AI-generated content becomes more prevalent, questions about authenticity, representation, and identity will come to the forefront, challenging traditional notions of creativity, authorship, and ownership. Moreover, the democratization of content creation afforded by VLOGGER AI has the potential to amplify diverse voices, foster community engagement, and empower marginalized communities, leading to more inclusive and participatory media landscapes.

Chapter 12: Societal Impacts and Cultural Shifts

In the ever-evolving landscape of technology, the societal impacts and cultural shifts brought about by innovations like VLOGGER AI are profound and far-reaching. This exploration delves into the multifaceted ways in which VLOGGER AI is shaping our society, influencing cultural norms, and driving significant shifts in how we create, consume, and interact with digital content.

Redefining Creativity and Authorship

One of the most notable societal impacts of VLOGGER AI is its redefinition of creativity and authorship. With the ability to generate lifelike avatars and dynamic content autonomously, VLOGGER AI challenges traditional notions of artistic expression and ownership. Creators no longer need to be bound by their physical limitations or technical skills; instead, they can leverage VLOGGER AI to bring their ideas to life in ways that were previously unimaginable. This democratization of creativity has the potential to empower individuals from diverse backgrounds and perspectives, fostering a more inclusive and collaborative creative culture.

Amplifying Diversity and Representation

Another significant societal impact of VLOGGER AI is its role in amplifying diversity and representation in digital media. By enabling users to create personalized avatars that reflect their identities and experiences, VLOGGER AI promotes greater visibility and inclusion of underrepresented groups in online spaces. This has the potential to challenge stereotypes, break down barriers, and foster a more inclusive and equitable digital environment. Moreover, VLOGGER AI can be used to generate content in multiple languages, dialects, and cultural contexts, facilitating cross-cultural communication and understanding on a global scale.

Reducing Barriers to Content Creation

VLOGGER AI has the potential to significantly reduce barriers to content creation, democratizing access to digital media production tools and resources. Historically, creating high-quality video content required specialized skills, equipment, and resources, making it inaccessible to many individuals, particularly those from marginalized communities. However, with VLOGGER AI, anyone with a smartphone or computer can easily generate professional-looking videos and animations using simple voice commands or gestures. This democratization of content creation not only empowers individuals to share their stories and perspectives but also fosters greater diversity and creativity in the digital landscape.

Challenging Ethical and Moral Norms

As VLOGGER AI becomes more sophisticated and pervasive, it raises important ethical and moral questions about the authenticity and integrity of digital content. The rise of deepfake technology, which uses AI to manipulate audio and video recordings to create deceptive or misleading content, has sparked concerns about the spread of misinformation, identity theft, and privacy violations. Moreover, the use of AI-generated avatars in online interactions blurs the lines between reality and fiction, raising questions about consent, agency, and accountability. As society grapples with these complex ethical dilemmas, it is essential to establish clear guidelines and regulations to govern the responsible use of VLOGGER AI and ensure that it is deployed in ways that prioritize ethical considerations and uphold fundamental human rights.

Shaping New Forms of Communication and Expression

VLOGGER AI is also shaping new forms of communication and expression in the digital age. From interactive storytelling experiences and immersive virtual worlds to personalized video messages and social media interactions, VLOGGER AI is expanding the possibilities for how we engage with digital media and connect with others online. This has the potential to revolutionize the way we communicate, collaborate, and build communities in both virtual and physical spaces. By harnessing the power of VLOGGER AI, individuals and organizations can create more engaging, meaningful, and impactful content that resonates with audiences on a deeper level.

Conclusion

As we reach the conclusion of our journey through the world of VLOGGER AI, it is evident that we stand on the precipice of a new era in content creation—one defined by innovation, creativity, and unprecedented technological advancement. Throughout this exploration, we have delved deep into the intricacies of VLOGGER AI, examining its genesis, functionality, limitations, and real-world applications. We have explored its transformative potential to revolutionize the way we create, consume, and interact with digital media, and we have grappled with the ethical, societal, and cultural implications of its widespread adoption.

In conclusion, the journey through the world of VLOGGER AI has been both enlightening and transformative. As we bid farewell to this exploration, let us carry forward the lessons learned and the insights gained, embracing the future with optimism, curiosity, and a commitment to ethical innovation. Let us continue to push the boundaries of creativity, challenge the status quo, and harness the power of technology to build a better, brighter future for all.

www.ingramcontent.com/pod-product-compliance
Lightning Source LLC
Chambersburg PA
CBHW070358230526
45471CB00006B/2620